"It's you, Super Sema! I should have known!" shouts Tobor. "Where's my elephant?" he demands.

"Where he belongs, Tobor—with his mama, in the wild," Super Sema replies.

Frustrated, Tobor tells her, "One day A.I. shall triumph forever!" But the elephants trumpet in reply!

"That's 'never' in elephant." Sema giggles, glad to have saved the day once again.

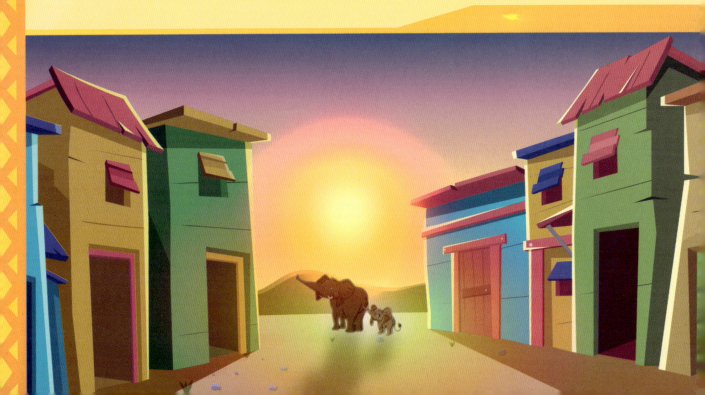

After sliding down, Baby Tembo cries—this time with joy, happily reunited with his mother!

Moyo has a brilliant idea! With Baby Tembo's help, they pour water down the steep bank, turning it into a fun mudslide for Baby Tembo!

Outside, Sema and her family spot Baby Tembo's mom in the distance, running toward them. The plan worked; she heard her baby's cries! But now there's a new problem—how will they get the little elephant down from Tobor's headquarters high on the hill before Tobor catches them?

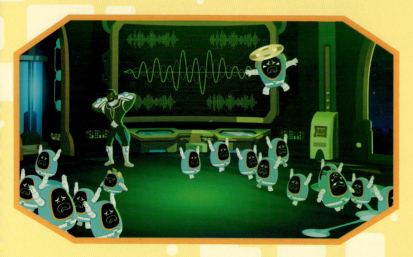

While Tobor tries to shut off the blaring sounds, Babu entices Baby Tembo out of the palace with more of Mrs. Tam Tam's delicious mandazi.

Sema and MB must move quickly now! MB switches the alarm over to the recording of Baby Tembo. The baby elephant's sad trumpets ring out through the speakers. "It's working!" he shouts excitedly.

At the sound of the alarm, Tobor and the Bongolalas wake up in a panic and storm the room. "What in Dunia is going on?!" Tobor shouts.

But while Sema's working, the real Baby Tembo keeps crying and Babu just can't bear it! He lets Baby Tembo out too early—setting off the alarms by mistake. Oh no!

Sema sneaks off to connect the recording to Tobor's speaker system.

But soon, while Tobor and the Bongolalas are sleeping, Sema and her family tiptoe into his palace to find the little elephant and secretly record his cries. Success!

Back at his headquarters, Tobor quickly realizes that rambunctious Baby Tembo is not an obedient pet that he can train to carry him around the streets of Dunia like a king. So Tobor locks Baby Tembo away instead. Poor Baby Tembo!

Soon Sema, MB, Babu, and Moyo are off to save Baby Tembo!

They continue their research and discover that a mother elephant will travel for miles if she hears her baby's cry. That gives Sema a brilliant idea!

"Let's technovate!" they all shout. Then they get to work.

"What will happen if Baby Tembo doesn't find his mother again?" Sema asks.

"I'm afraid he won't survive," Babu tells her sadly.

"We've got to save him!" Sema insists. "There must be a way!"

Sema and MB run up to their lab and get to work researching all about elephants to try and find a way to save Baby Tembo. "Baby elephants need their mothers for milk and protection," MB reads on his computer. "Sometimes for up to ten years!"

With the help of his army of Bongolalas, Tobor steals Baby Tembo right out from under Sema and Moyo's noses!

Meanwhile, evil Tobor spots Baby Tembo with his telescoping cyber-eye. "Now that is a pet for a powerful ruler. I must have that baby elephant! It shall be mine!"

At home, Moyo is nervous about inviting an elephant into their house! Baby Tembo trumpets through the kitchen looking for food and then slides and splashes in the mud outside, making just as big a mess as he did in the marketplace!

Even though Moyo now thinks he's adorable, the family quickly realizes that the spunky little elephant needs to return to the wild.

"It's just a baby tembo, Mrs. Tam Tam," Sema's grandpa Babu says. Using Mrs. Tam Tam's delicious mandazi treats, he convinces the adorable baby elephant to leave the marketplace and follow them home.

Tembo is "elephant" in Swahili.

"It's an elephant!" explains Mrs. Tam Tam, as Baby Tembo splashes her and Peter Pizza with squashed fruit. "He's destroying everything! Can you get him out of here?"

"Shoo! Get away!" shout Mrs. Tam Tam and Peter Pizza alongside the scared townspeople.

"What's happening?!" asks Sema.

One beautiful morning in Dunia, Sema, MB, and Babu arrive at the marketplace to find a huge mess!

Tembo the Baby Elephant

**based on the episode "Tembo the Baby Elephant" written by Claudia Lloyd
adapted by Sarah Jospitre**

PENGUIN YOUNG READERS LICENSES
An imprint of Penguin Random House LLC
1745 Broadway, New York, New York, 10019

First published in the United States of America by Penguin Young Readers Licenses, an imprint of Penguin Random House LLC, 2024

Super Sema™ and associated characters, trademarks, and design elements are owned and licensed by Kukua Education Limited.
© 2024 Kukua Education Limited. All Rights Reserved.

Penguin supports copyright. Copyright fuels creativity, encourages diverse voices, promotes free speech, and creates a vibrant culture. Thank you for buying an authorized edition of this book and for complying with copyright laws by not reproducing, scanning, or distributing any part of it in any form without permission. You are supporting writers and allowing Penguin to continue to publish books for every reader.

Visit us online at penguinrandomhouse.com.

Manufactured in China

ISBN 9780593752708

10 9 8 7 6 5 4 3 2 1 HH